This brochure shows you the way to the most impressive works of art in the Our Lady's Cathedral of Antwerp. At the same time, it offers explanatory information about all of these works. Religious information. Art-historical information. Historical information. Technical information. In this way, too, you can easily find your way to the meaning and background of the art selected.

Unfold the cover flap and use both sides in combination with the rest of the brochure.

A few introductory pages contain general information. About the stirring history of the Cathedral, among other things, and about Peter Paul Rubens, four masterly paintings by whom hang in crucial places in the Cathedral.

History of the Our Lady's Cathedral

The Our Lady's Cathedral of Antwerp reconciles 'being' with 'becoming'. For five centuries, its north tower, which points toward God like a finger, has dominated the silhouette of the city without changing. But during that same period, the Cathedral was repaired and refurnished repeatedly. It assembles the various styles of the times - gothic, renaissance, baroque, rococo, and so on - without ever taking on a definitive form.

The Cathedral harbors, for example, a marble statue of the madonna from the fourteenth century. Some of the wall paintings date from the fifteenth century. The stately devotional statue 'Our Lady of Antwerp' in the Mary chapel is sixteenth century. The four baroque masterpieces by Rubens first saw the light of day in the beginning of the seventeenth century. A tabernacle in the form of the Ark of the Covenant, just like the large clock on the tower above, is eighteenth century. The neogothic decoration stems from the nineteenth century. The sculptures that decorate the main portal were added at the beginning of the twentieth century. And as recently as 1993, a Metzler organ was installed above the south entrance to the ambulatory.

For more than a thousand years now, Antwerp Catholics have honored and revered Our Lady, who is the patroness of both Antwerp and the Cathedral. Where the Cathedral now stands, there was a small chapel of Our Lady from the ninth to the twelfth century, which acquired the status of parish church in 1124. During the course of the twelfth century, it was replaced by a larger Romanesque church. From wall and foundation remains, it appears that this church was 80 meters long and 42 meters wide, and must have looked something like St. Maria im Kapitol in Cologne.

In 1352, construction was begun on a new church which would become the largest gothic church in the Netherlands. In the beginning, it was to be provided with two towers of equal height.

In 1521, after nearly 170 years, the Church of Our Lady was ready. The south tower reached only as far as the third string course. After the new church was largely gutted by fire during the night of October 5-6, 1533, all energy and means went into its repair. The completion of the second tower was delayed, which led to its ultimate postponement. Moreover,

ÆDES D. MARIÆ ANTVERPIÆ

the church only became the principal church of the bishopric of Antwerp, and hence a cathedral, in 1559, and lost this title again from 1801 to 1961 because the bishopric was abolished during this period.

As a building, the Our Lady's Cathedral, predominantly constructed in brick and white natural stone, is an impressive example of Brabant gothic. To its most important characteristics belong - in addition to the typical gothic pointed arches and large glazed windows - the decorative integration of architecture and sculpture, a sober and open interior architecture based on complex construction, spatial and vertical effects, and a subtle play of light and shadow. The church possesses a high north and a low south tower, an octagonal lantern- or crossing-tower with an onion-shaped dome, seven bays, a choir, transepts, an ambulatory, five radiating chapels and six side chapels. The north tower was under construction for a century, whereby its style evolved from robust high-gothic lower down to refined late-gothic higher up. The lowest masonry courses are heavy and square, with little ornamentation, while the tower above is progressively richer in decoration and more openly worked. The spire looks like stone lace.

The fire of 1533 is not the only disaster by which the Cathedral was visited. Only 33 years later, during the Iconoclasm of August 20, 1566, Protestants destroyed a large part of the valuable interior. When Antwerp came under Protestant administration in 1581, a number of artistic treasures were once again destroyed, removed or sold. Only after 1585, with the restoration of Roman Catholic authority, did tranquility return once more. Two centuries later another disaster presented itself. In 1794 the French revolutionaries conquered the region, whereupon they plundered the Our Lady's Cathedral and inflicted serious damage. Around 1798, the French administration even toyed with the idea of demolishing the building. But after each blow, the Cathedral was able to recover. In 1816, various important works of art were returned from Paris, among which three masterpieces by Rubens. And over the course of the ninetheenth century, the church was completely restored and refurnished. Between 1965 and 1993, another complete restoration took place.

Although the work never stops and a number of restoration projects are still in progress, the Our Lady's Cathedral is in excellent condition today. Naturally, it still serves as a church, as a place where the faithful experience their belief, but more than ever it is also a many-sided museum that attracts hundreds of thousands of visitors each year from all directions and all continents.

Numbers that count (and tell)

- The north tower of the Our Lady's Cathedral is 123 meters high, the south tower 65.30 meters, the central aisle 28 meters and the lantern- or crossing-tower where the nave and transepts meet 43 meters.

- On the interior, the Cathedral is 118 meters long. At the crossing, it is 67 meters wide. The maximum breadth of the nave is 53.50 meters.

- The total surface area of the floor is 8,000 square meters. At big events, 2,400 seats can be provided for. In principle, the Cathedral can hold 25,000 people.

- The surface area of the roof amounts to more than 10,000 square meters.

- The Cathedral has 7 bays, 125 columns and 128 windows (of which 55 are stained-glass).

- In the time of the guilds and trade associations, each of which had its own altar, there were 57 permanent altars distributed throughout the Cathedral.

- The nineteenth-century Schyven organ has 90 registers and 5,770 pipes.

- The Cathedral has a carillon with 49 bells at its disposal.

- Of the bells that can be rung, the Karolus, which dates from 1507 and weighs 6,434 kilograms, is the heaviest.

- Maintenance of the Cathedral costs 1.5 million euros per year.

- Every year, approximately 360,000 people visit the Cathedral.

Peter Paul Rubens (1577-1640)
the master of Flemish baroque

By bringing the nascent baroque style from Italy to Antwerp, Peter Paul Rubens radically renewed Flemish art of the seventeenth century. With his dynamic and sometimes frankly vertiginous pictorial representations that display a powerful imagination and at the same time an accurate realism, he quickly acquired international fame. He executed numerous artistic commissions not only for the church and for private citizens, but also for the archdukes Albert and Isabella, the Spanish kings Philip III and Philip IV, and the royal houses of England and France. Today, Rubens is counted among the greatest artists in history. In the Our Lady's Cathedral one can find four masterpieces by his hand: *The raising of the cross* (1609-1610), *The resurrection of Christ* (1611-1612), *The descent from the cross* (1611-1614) and *The assumption of the Virgin* (1625-1626).

Born in Westphalia on June 28, 1577, the son of an Antwerp lawyer, Peter Paul Rubens only arrived in Antwerp after the death of his father in 1587. He was trained as a painter and became a 'free master' in 1598. From 1600 to 1608, he perfected himself as an artist in Italy, where he studied the sculptures of classical antiquity and the works of famous renaissance artists like Michelangelo, Raphael and Titian, and was influenced by the baroque paintings of Caravaggio.

Upon his return to Antwerp in 1609, Rubens became court painter to the Spanish regents Albert and Isabella. That same year he married Isabella Brant and in 1610 established himself in a house on the Wapper, which he built up into a flourishing atelier with palatial allure. Working with various assistant painters, including Anthony Van Dyck, he painted many religious and mythological works there, and a number of portraits as well. The accent lay on monumental, lively art that paired an outspoken dramatic emotionality with surprising harmony.

The paintings that Rubens made after his fortieth birthday look more controlled, although movement and feeling still occupy an important place in them. His palette evolved toward light, warm colors. In 1620, Rubens made a series of ceiling paintings for the Antwerp Jesuit church (the present-day Church of Carolus Borromeus), which in 1718 would be destroyed by fire. He also painted an impressive cycle of 25 scenes from the life of the French queen Maria de Medici, enriched by allegorical elements, in the period from 1621 to 1625. In 1626, his wife died, but four years later the 53-year-old artist married Helena Fourment, then barely 16 years old.

Between 1623 and 1633, Rubens regularly served as a diplomat. Thus he lay at the origin of the peace accord that was concluded between England and Spain in 1630, an effort for which the English king Charles I knighted him. But his diplomatic activities did not spell the end of his artistic career. At the request of Charles I, Rubens made a series of ceiling paintings for Whitehall Palace in London between 1629 and 1635. Afterward, on the orders of Philip IV, he painted more than one hundred works for the Torre de la Parada, the hunting lodge of the Spanish king near Madrid.

During the last ten years of his life Rubens, who after 1635 lived chiefly at his estate Het Steen near Elewijt, devoted himself increasingly to landscapes and genre paintings. By elegantly weaving mythical and realistic elements with each other and by using light coloring, he was able to make of them an extraordinarily enchanting whole. His art became more lyrical and less dramatic.

On May 30, 1640, the great master of Flemish baroque died from an attack of gout. His mortal body is buried in the St James Church, but his immortal paintings are still to be admired - among other places in the Our Lady's Cathedral.

① *Sculpture*
'Madonna and child'
Master of the Marble Madonnas

The loveliness and refined elegance of this standing madonna and child (127 x 40 x 27 cm) connect seamlessly with the court culture of the fourteenth century, when an anonymous artist carved the statue from a lump of Carrara marble. The mannered representation - the perfect S-shape of Mary's posture, the considered way in which her clothing and that of the infant Jesus fall in stylish folds - does not prevent the whole from radiating a sensitivity and authenticity which even after nearly seven centuries still softens hearts immediately. Among other things, Mary's quiet smile is striking. The apparently spontaneous gesture of the little Jesus, who strokes his mother's cheek with the tiny fingers of his right hand, only increases its charm.
It is quite probable that it is an important work by a Liege sculptor, who is called the 'Master of the Marble Madonnas'.

② *Devotional statue*
'Our Lady of Antwerp'
Anonymous

That this is, not coincidentally, the Our Lady's Cathedral and that reverence for the Virgin has always been quite popular in Antwerp shows in the stately, lustrous decoration of the amply dimensioned Mary chapel. More even than the imposing altar, the many candelabras, the silverwork and the three nineteenth-century stained-glass windows dedicated to Our Lady, the 180 cm sixteenth-century devotional statue of Mary with Jesus on her arm functions as an eye-catcher here. Mother and child are represented at their most royal: both with a large gold scepter and crown, which are moreover set with precious stones. The garments look just as majestic. In addition, Mary and Jesus are regularly dressed in other clothing, because they have at their disposal a wardrobe that is fantastic in every respect. Because of its rather ceremonial character, this painted wooden image evokes reverence and awe. Which is also fitting, because in the Mary chapel the faithful pray to Our Lady in her capacity as ruler of heaven, in the hope of acquiring her blessing and favor.

Painting
'The raising of the cross'
Peter Paul Rubens

Rubens (1577-1640) painted *The raising of the cross* in 1609-1610, when he himself was about the age of the martyred Christ. Until 1794, this colossal work (central panel: 460 x 340 cm, side panels: 460 x 150 cm) was part of the high altar of the St Walburgis Church, which was later demolished. Hauled away by the French, the triptych was returned to Antwerp in 1815, where since 1816 it has had a central place in the Our Lady's Cathedral. In *The raising of the cross*, Rubens introduced baroque art in the Netherlands after an eight year stay in Italy. The whirling strength, the impelling dynamism that characterize this masterpiece full of drama and pathos are striking. Nevertheless the whole presentation appears coherent and balanced. The diagonal composition of the *central panel*, with nine assistant executioners who act in unison, exerting their intensely earthly, carnal strength to raise the cross with the pale Christ, possesses a gruesome beauty. Here, Rubens has set down the raising of the cross, which until that time had scarcely appeared in the visual arts, in an unprecedentedly expressive, almost tempestuous manner. This relates to Roman-Catholic self-confidence, which was regained during the Counterreformation.

On the *left panel*, John and Mary (above) observe the disconcerting
event with a number of mourning women (below). On the *right panel*, a
mounted Roman commander directs the crucifixion. In the background,
the two thieves who are to die with Christ can be seen: while one thief
is being undressed, the other has already been crucified.

The four saints on the *reverse of the side panels* refer to the original
destination of the painting. They are Amandus (according to tradition
the founder of the St Walburgis Church), Walburgis herself, Eligius (the
patron saint of the Antwerp smiths, who had their guild altar in the
St Walburgis Church) and Catherine (who was the object of a special
devotion in the church).

④ **Stained-glass window with the archdukes Albert and Isabella in adoration of the cross**
Cornelis Cussers / Jan Baptist van der Veken

In 1598 the archdukes Albert and Isabella served as rulers of the South Netherlands. After the turbulent sixteenth century, with its bitter conflict between Catholics and Protestants, tranquility returned to Antwerp under the restored Spanish Catholic administration. In 1609, Albert and Isabella concluded a twelve-year truce with the Protestant North Netherlands. The Counterreformation was flourishing under their rule. The Roman Catholic churches were repaired, restored and richly redecorated. So, too, was the Our Lady's Cathedral, which was in the first place provided with various unparalleled paintings by Peter Paul Rubens, who in 1609 became court painter to the archdukes.
In this stained-glass window in the north wall of the transept, made in 1616 by Cornelis Cussers(? - ca 1617) after a design by Jan Baptist van der Veken, Albert (right) and Isabella are portrayed while they kneel in prayer before the crucified Christ. Both are accompanied by their patron saints, respectively bishop Albert the Great (with miter) and Elisabeth of Thüringen (with crown). Behind the four figures is a strikingly large round arch offering a view of a church, which may depict the basilica of Scherpenheuvel, which was zealously being constructed on the orders of Albert and Isabella when this stained-glass window first saw the light of day. That many Antwerp natives believed that Our Lady of Scherpenheuvel had saved their city from a plague epidemic in 1603 may have been an additional reason for referring to the basilica.

5 'Angel-throne' in gilt and silvered wood
Mattheus van Beveren / Artus Quellinus the Younger

This wooden exposition- or sacrament-throne (300 x 195 x 89 cm), better
known as the 'angel-throne', is an interesting example of the late
baroque. Characteristic for that style is the elegant mobility of the
figures. The throne was made for the choir of the Cathedral in 1659-1660
by Mattheus van Beveren (1630-1690), after a design by Artus Quellinus
the Younger (1625-1700). In 1660-1661, the work was gilt and silvered.
Together, two standing and two hovering angels hold up a large crown
made from ears of grain and hung with clusters of grapes. The grain and
the grapes refer to the bread and the wine, which in turn refer to the
body and blood of Christ, and hence to the Eucharist. The pelican with its
young depicted on the socle is also a eucharistic symbol. On the actual
socle stands a smaller socle for the monstrance.

6 St Joseph retable
Jean-Baptist de Boeck / Jean-Baptist van Wint / Louis Hendrix

In the period between 1870 and 1873, the entire St Joseph chapel was decorated in the neogothic style. And the beautiful St Joseph retable (centerpiece: 245 x 272 cm, side panels: 245 x 136 cm) also dates from this time. The retable stands proudly on a painted stone altar table (132.5 x 292 x 137.5 cm) that rests on four small columns in front and behind on a slab decorated with three coats of arms. The centerpiece consists of finely carved woodwork by Jean-Baptist de Boeck (1826-1902) and Jean-Baptist van Wint (ca 1835-1906). With care and craftsmanship, they have portrayed St Joseph - who carries the Christ child on his arm - and seven episodes from his life. To the left of the central St Joseph sculpture, from top to bottom, are the marriage of Joseph and Mary, the birth of Christ, and the presentation of Jesus in the temple; to the right, the flight into Egypt, Jesus found in the temple of Jerusalem, and the Holy Family in Nazareth. The scene in the center below refers to the death of Joseph.

The paintings on the side panels of the retable are by the hand of Louis Hendrix (1827-1888). At the upper left, a kneeling pope Pius IX and his patron saint, Peter, are represented; below, saints Bernard of Siena, Thomas Aquinas, John of Chrysostome, Augustine and Jerome. At the upper right, a kneeling king Charles II and the sainted bishop Maternus are visible; below, saints Birgitta of Sweden, Theresa, Ignatius of Loyola, Frances of Sales, Vincent de Paul and Alphonse.

⑦ *Painting*
'The death of the Virgin'
Abraham Matthyssens

Surrounded by the apostles, among others, and three women who -
according to legend - laid her to rest after her death, the still young-
looking Mary, who shows no sign of suffering, lies on her deathbed. The
uppermost part of the painting shows Christ and the angels preparing
themselves for her imminent arrival in heaven. The angels have Marian
symbols with them to honor the mother of God.
The death of the Virgin, painted in 1633 by Rubens' contemporary
Abraham Matthyssens (1581-1649), is a striking example of triumphalism
in Flemish art during the Counterreformation. Roman Catholicism could
breathe freely again; quiet devotion was to some extent supplanted by
the jubilant experience and proclamation of faith. A degree of this
triumphalism is certainly to be found in the work of Rubens as well.
In the Cathedral, the large canvas (500 x 325 cm) by Matthyssens hangs
on the reverse side of the high altar, on the back, as it were, of the
assumption of the Virgin painted by Rubens (see page 21), with which it
forms, along with the painting in the cupola by Cornelis Schut (see page
30), an obvious thematic unity.

⑧ Tomb of bishop Marius Ambrosius Capello
Artus Quellinus the Younger

With legs drawn up and upper body resting on his elbow, his mitered head turned upward and hands folded in prayer, bishop Marius Ambrosius Capello (1597-1676) lies on his marble tomb, depicted life-size (sarcophagus and socle: 120 x 205 x 82 cm, statue: 123 x 205 x 60 cm). This is the only one of the five tombs of former bishops of the Our Lady's Cathedral that has been preserved. Until the arrival of the French at the end of the eighteenth century, all of the tombs were in the choir.
Capello's baroque tomb in white, black and red marble was made with attention to the smallest detail by Artus Quellinus the Younger (1625-1700). It bears witness to a lively creativity and couples realism with idealization.
Bishop Capello was highly regarded and was also beloved by the poor people of Antwerp, to whom he left all of his possessions. Out of thankfulness for this act, the almoners of the city had a large commemorative monument made for him shortly after his death. It still hangs in the nave of the Cathedral towards the front, against one of the supporting walls of the south tower.

⑨ Fragments of a wall painting depicting the Man of Sorrows
Anonymous

Intriguing discoveries are occasionally made in the Our Lady's Cathedral. Thus, in 1989-1990, in the chapel where the tomb of bishop Capello (see page 19) stands, a fragment of a wall painting was exposed that depicted the risen Christ showing his wounds. The Man of Sorrows, as such representations of Christ are called, is located to the left of the entrance to the sacristy and dates from the beginning of the fifteenth century. He belongs to a larger group of paintings that once decorated all of the chapel walls and two pillars of the ambulatory but are now hidden from view by later decorative layers.

In the meantime, the pierced feet of the Man of Sorrows have also been uncovered, which permits a better look at the entire work of art. Christ is portrayed life-size and provided with a crown of thorns, plus a halo in the form of a gold-colored disc. It is telling that he stands on an altar with a chalice between his feet, above which the host hovers. The whole work refers explicitly to the then-current theme of the mass of St Gregory. In order to remove doubts as to the real presence of Christ during the Eucharist, Christ himself is supposed to have appeared to pope Gregory during the aforementioned mass as the Man of Sorrows.

'The assumption of the Virgin'
Peter Paul Rubens

10 *Painting*
'The assumption of the Virgin'
Peter Paul Rubens

It is evident that the imposing oil painting (490 x 325 cm), which has adorned the high altar for nearly four hundred years, is dedicated to the patroness of the Cathedral. That it depicts the assumption of the Virgin is also self-evident. Although the theme derives from church tradition and is not based on the Bible itself, it was nevertheless especially popular when Rubens made this altarpiece in 1625-1626. Borne up by a cloud of playful cherubs, light as a feather, with fluttering hair and gown, eyes expectantly turned toward heaven, Mary rises upward from her stone tomb. To the left, two large angels fly in to crown her with a garland of roses. Below, near the abandoned grave, are the twelve apostles and the three women who according to legend were present at Mary's death.

Over the years, Rubens sketched and painted the assumption of Mary several times. As far as the composition is concerned, all of these assumptions are closely related, but none of them exceeds the swirling beauty and subtle play of light and color of this panel.

Rubens also designed the gigantic new marble high altar with columns that originally framed the panel. That altar was, however, destroyed by the French at the end of the eighteenth century. In 1824, another stately new high altar was installed which in 1993 acquired its present somewhat smaller, lower form.

'The resurrection of Christ'
Peter Paul Rubens

11 *Painting*
'The resurrection of Christ'
Peter Paul Rubens

For the married couple Jan Moretus and Martina Plantin, of the
renowned Antwerp Plantin-Moretus family of printers, Rubens painted
this commemorative triptych in 1611-12 (central panel: 138 x 98 cm,
side panels: 136 x 40 cm). Jan Moretus died in 1610. His widow, who
commissioned the work, lived until 1616.
The *central panel* (see page 23) shows Christ, to the alarm of the
soldiers shrinking back in the darkness, strong and radiantly rising from
his rocky tomb. This type of tomb was a novelty, since up until then it
had been the practice in art to portray the tomb of Christ as a sarcophagus.
On the *side panels*, Rubens has portrayed John the Baptist and
St Martina, the patron saints of Jan and Martina Moretus. John stands
on the bank of the Jordan; the sword on the ground refers to his
beheading. St Martina holds a palm branch in her hand as a sign of her
martyrdom. Behind her, one can see the broken fragments of the temple
of the sun god Apollo, which is supposed to have collapsed when
Martina made the sign of the cross.
For the depiction of various figures in this triptych, Rubens was inspired
by sculptures from antiquity. This is true for Christ and St Martina, and
certainly also for the beautiful angels on the *reverse of the side panels*.
The angels stand with their backs to a double door, which they seem
about to open. Is it the door to eternal life?

 Choir-stall
François Durlet

It will come as no surprise that the nineteenth-century neogothic choir-stall of the Our Lady's Cathedral was designed by an architect, because it has a lot in common with a cathedral. With two oak cathedrals, actually, placed opposite one another, each with a central tower and 36 seats. The architect in question was named François Durlet (1816-1867). He was only 23 years old when his design, submitted on the occasion of a competition, took the prize. That design marked the beginning of a far-reaching neogothic refurnishing and redecoration of the Cathedral, which was only completed at the beginning of the twentieth century and behind which Durlet was the directing and driving force until his death. The completion of this monumental choir-stall took more than forty years, from 1840 to 1883. A whole series of well-known sculptors worked on its countless decorative and figurative parts. Of particular note are the 36 episodes from the life of Our Lady, depicted in high relief. A number of free-standing sculptures also belong to the choir-stall, which is used by the canons of the Cathedral. They depict, among other things, saints, angels, apostles, prophets and symbolic figures. For security reasons, most of these statues are not on display.

'The descent from the cross'
Peter Paul Rubens

13 *Painting*
'The descent from the cross'
Peter Paul Rubens

Although painted a few years after *The raising of the cross*, Rubens to some extent made use of another style for *The descent from the cross* (1611-1614). The sense of clarity and serenity are greater here. The light shines more softly. The positions and movements of the figures are more controlled. Overall, the whole painting looks more classical. Nevertheless, because of its stylish grandeur, monumental character (central panel: 421 x 311 cm, side panels: 421 x 153 cm), diagonal composition, and sense of the dramatic and decorative, this triptych is a paragon of baroque art.

On the *central panel* (see page 27) eight people carefully take the lifeless Christ from the cross. Starting from the top and moving down, there are two anonymous helpers, then Joseph of Arimathea on the left and Nicodemus on the right; below are Mary, who stretches out her arms toward her son, John, in his fiery red garments, and at the very bottom Mary Cleophas and Mary Magdalen. Against the flat, dark background the figures light up three-dimensionally, as it were. Together they bear the body of Christ, which they have taken up in a white shroud - a reference to the Corpus Christi and the Eucharist.

The bearing of Christ is a theme repeated throughout this triptych. The *left panel* shows Mary, who is expecting, visiting her also-pregnant cousin Elizabeth, who will bring John the Baptist into the world. The two women are accompanied by their husbands, Joseph and Zacharias. On the *right panel* Mary has just handed the infant Jesus to the high priest Simeon. Joseph kneels before Simeon and holds in his hand two doves intended as offerings.

The *reverse of the side panels* refers to the medieval legend of Saint Christopher, a name that literally means 'Christ bearer'. Supporting himself on a stick, Christopher must exert himself to the extreme in order to be able to carry the unexpectedly heavy child Jesus on his back. To the right, a hermit shows him the way in the dark with a lamp. Saint Christopher was the patron saint of the Antwerp musketeers, the military guild that ordered *The descent from the cross* from Rubens in 1611 for their altar in the Our Lady's Cathedral. Which immediately explains the presence of the saint and all the allusions to the bearing of Christ in this triptych.

14 *Painting*
'The assumption of the Virgin'
Cornelis Schut

Where the central aisle and transepts intersect, there hangs a breathtaking circular painting on canvas (diameter: 580 cm), 43 meters above the ground in the so-called crossing-tower of the Cathedral. It portrays Mary, who, encircled by a swirling multitude of angels and cherubs, rises toward heaven in a radiant light. In just a few moments she will be with God the Father and God the Son, who, it is true, are only visible to Cathedral visitors with a telescope and who together hold the crown they will place upon her head. The Holy Ghost, the third member of the Holy Trinity, also waits for Mary in the form of a dove. The Antwerp artist Cornelis Schut (1597-1655) completed this work in 1647. Along with his sublime use of light and dark, the perspective is also worthy of note. Basing himself on Italian baroque vault and cupola painting, Schut reproduced the assumption from the point of view of people standing on the ground. The painting extends the crossing tower to infinity, as it were, and provides the viewer with the overwhelming sensation of looking straight up into heaven.

In addition, a few dozen meters below, a design for the painting (diameter: 82 cm) made just before 1647, which very strongly resembles the final version of the work, hangs on one of the crossing piers.

The assumption of the Virgin by Cornelis Schut is the final piece in a monumental three-part cycle in honor of the patroness of the Cathedral. The cycle further includes *The death of the Virgin* by Abraham Matthyssens (see page 18) and the assumption painted by Rubens (see page 21). In the work by Rubens, the beginning of her ascent can be seen; in that of Schut, the mother of God has almost reached her heavenly destination.

⑮ Silver antependium of the central altar of the crossing
Jan Pieter Antoon Verschuylen

In 1865 the Antwerp silversmith Jan Pieter Antoon Verschuylen made this antependium (literally: something that hangs in front), which now adorns the central altar in the crossing. Originally it was intended for the Shoemaker's chapel on the Schoenmarkt (or shoe market), where Verschuylen was a director.

Surrounded by acanthus leaves, cherub heads and roses, the glorious birth of the Virgin Mary is portrayed. The text on the banderole held tightly by two angels leaves no doubt: 'Nativitas Gloriosae / Virginis Mariae'. The antependium has a scalloped border adorned with roses and other plant-like embellishments.

16 Tabernacle in the form of the Ark of the Covenant
Judocus Ignatius Picavet / Hendrik Frans Verbrugghen /
Henricus II de Potter

This gilt wooden tabernacle (200 x 132 x 85 cm) decorated with
reliefs in gilt brass is shaped like the Ark of the Covenant in the Old
Testament. That ark symbolizes the alliance of God with the people of
Israel. It was made at the command of Moses, who kept in it the tablets
of the law that he had received on Mount Sinai. Later, it was supposed
to have stood in the temple in Jerusalem, after which it vanished
without a trace.

The tabernacle, designed in a rococo style by the sculptor Hendrik Frans
Verbrugghen (1654-1724) around 1710, has a vaulted cover and two
wooden rods for carrying and is adorned on three sides with chased
reliefs depicting the Eucharist. The two reliefs on the narrow sides were
made in 1712 by the Antwerp gold- and silversmith Judocus Ignatius
Picavet (1674-1729). On one panel, Moses proudly holds the tablets of
the law, while manna from heaven falls before his people; the other
depicts Elias, who received bread and water from an angel in the desert.
The relief on the front side was only made later, by the Brussels gold-
and silversmith Henricus II de Potter (1725-1781), and show the meeting
between Abraham and the priest-king Melchizedek, both accompanied
by soldiers. The Bible tells of how Abraham received bread and wine
from Melchizedek and was blessed by him.

In the Cathedral, this noteworthy tabernacle has been given a place in
the large Venerabelkapel (Sacrament chapel). There, it stands on the
altar of the Brotherhood of the Most Holy Sacrament, for whom it was
also made.

17 Pulpit
Michiel van der Voort

This oak pulpit, which was made by Michiel van der Voort (1667-1737) in
1713 for the St Bernard Abbey in Hemiksem, is richer in meaning than
some sermons. It has been in the Our Lady's Cathedral since 1804.
The banisters in the form of stems, branches and twigs, as well as the
trees that hold up the sound-board that covers the casket, look very
realistic. Indeed, so do the birds (among which are a parrot, a crane
and a small owl) and other animals who have found a place in the lush
vegetation. According to St Bernard, nature was an important source of
inspiration for the faithful, and the pulpit recalls it vividly.
The base on which the casket rests consists of four female figures, each
embodying a continent: Europe, Asia, America and Africa. Indeed, the
word of God was to be spread across the whole of the then-known
world. On the baroque casket itself the faces of Christ, Mary and
St Bernard are depicted in relief.
The cherubs at the edge of the sound-board in rococo style create the
impression that they carry the board up with them. In a halo of light
the Holy Ghost, present as a white dove, spreads its wings, while at
the very top a large angel trumpets the Joyous Message.
In spite of the mix of styles - naturalism, baroque, rococo - this pulpit
forms an unmistakable whole that belongs to the pinnacle of Flemish
sculpture.

⑱ Confessionals
Guillielmus Ignatius(?) Kerricx / Michiel van der Voort

Against the north wall of the nave of the Cathedral stand three groups
of oak confessionals which belong to the most splended made in
Antwerp around 1700. Of particular note are the 24 life size sculptures
that stand before the partitions. On one side are the twelve apostles,
and on the other, twelve women representing various virtues,
such as Contrition (a woman with a whip, a fish and a pelican), the
Enlightenment of Conscience (a woman with a torch) and Divine Mercy
(a woman with a horn of plenty).
The ensembles, which each consist of two 'open' confessionals, are
artistically worked overall. Note the large medallions with portraits of
Christ and the saints, for example, and the friezes embellished with
flowers and cherubs.
These confessionals, just like the pulpit at the side of the central aisle
(see page 33), probably came from the St Bernard Abbey in Hemiksem.
They were presumably made by Guillielmus Ignatius Kerricx (1682-1745)
and Michiel van der Voort (1667-1737).

19 *Painting*
'The Holy Family with angels'
Hendrik van Balen

While Mary, Joseph and the infant Jesus pause during the flight to Egypt, angels provide them with food and drink. The dove at the top of the painting represents the Holy Ghost. The young boy that hands a basket of plums and olives to Jesus is John the Baptist. This is confirmed by the camel-hair shirt, the small lamb to the right of the boy and the cross on the ground. Yet, however idyllic the scene may look at first glance, a shadow of Christ's future suffering nevertheless falls across it. The olives in the painting probably refer to the Mount of Olives and the Olive Garden, and the nails and other instruments of the passion that some of the angels have with them announce unequivocally Jesus' eventual death as a martyr.

This is in fact only the central panel (180 x 122 cm) of a triptych that was painted by Hendrik van Balen (1575-1632) shortly after 1622 for the grave of the merchant Filip Heemsen and his wife Anna van Eelen. Hendrik van Balen was the teacher of Anthony Van Dyck, among others.

⑳ Schyven organ case
Peter Verbrugghen the Elder / Michel Boursoy /
Erasmus Quellinus the Younger

The Our Lady's Cathedral has two organs. The new Metzler organ (1993), located above the south entrance to the ambulatory, was built for the performance of the organ compositions of Bach and his French contemporaries. The older, romantic Schyven organ (1891) permits the organ music of the nineteenth and twentieth centuries to achieve its proper splendor.
The enormous baroque wooden case of the Schyven organ is much older than the organ itself. It dates from 1657 and was made according to a design by the painter Erasmus Quellinus the Younger by Peter Verbrugghen the Elder, who carved the figures, and Michel Boursoy, who took care of the ornamentation. Above, an eminently appropriate St Cecilia, patroness of music, with a partiture in her lap and a small organ at her right, sits enthroned in a niche in the center. Below St Cecilia, four large angels make music. She is flanked by cherubs and an angel with a trumpet stands above her as well. The actual instrument was built by Brussels native Pierre Schyven, and has four keyboards and pedals, 90 registers and 5,770 pipes.